CASCADIA SCORECARD 2007

CASCADIA SCORECARD

SEVEN KEY TRENDS SHAPING THE NORTHWEST

2007

Sightline
INSTITUTE

SIGHTLINE INSTITUTE (formerly Northwest Environment Watch) is a not-for-profit research and communication center—a think tank—based in Seattle. Its mission is to bring about sustainability: a healthy, lasting prosperity grounded in place. Sightline is nonpartisan and wholly independent; its only ideology is commitment to the shared values of strong communities, fair markets, and responsible stewardship. Its focus is Cascadia, or the Pacific Northwest.

Library of Congress Control Number: 2007903046
ISBN 1-886093-17-2
(ISBN-13: 978-1-886093-17-1)

Design, production, and illustration: Jennifer Shontz
Editing: Nicholas H. Allison
Proofreading: Sherri Schultz

Printed by Transcontinental Printing, Canada, with vegetable-based ink on recycled paper. Text pages 100 percent postconsumer waste, bleached without chlorine; map pages 10 percent postconsumer, bleached without chlorine.

Sightline Institute is a 501(c)(3) tax-exempt organization. To order publications, become a member, or learn more, please contact:

Sightline Institute
1402 Third Avenue, Suite 500
Seattle, WA 98101-2130 USA
(206) 447-1880; fax (206) 447-2270
www.sightline.org

CONTENTS

CASCADIA AND
ITS SCORECARD

This book begins with place: Cascadia, the Pacific Northwest. Encompassing British Columbia, Idaho, Washington, Oregon, and adjoining parts of Alaska, Montana, and California (see map inside front cover), Cascadia is a region with a dawning sense of itself. Its population is larger than the Netherlands', its economy is larger than Russia's, and its land area is larger than France, Germany, and the United Kingdom combined—with Belgium, Italy, and Switzerland thrown in for good measure.

Named for the Cascade Mountains, for the earthquake-prone Cascadia subduction zone offshore under the Pacific, and—above all—for the cascading waterfalls that pepper the region, Cascadia has a common indigenous cultural heritage and a common history. It is bound by salmon and rivers, snowcapped mountains and towering forests. Its people share not only geography but also an aspiration: to live well in their place.

Cascadia has a tradition of innovation in the public and private sectors, a well-educated populace, and a long-standing commitment to conservation and quality of life. These traits show: the Northwest retains a larger share of its natural heritage intact than perhaps any other part of the industrial world. It has helped set the conservation agenda for the continent.

Still, Cascadians are in only the early phases of rising to the next great challenge for humanity: gradually but fundamentally realigning the human enterprise so that both the economy and its supporting ecosystems can thrive. Daunting, complex, systemic, seemingly quixotic, this goal—a healthy, lasting prosperity—is nonetheless more attainable here than anywhere else on this continent. If northwesterners can reconcile themselves with their landscapes, they can set an example for the world.

Cascadia's people share not only geography but also an aspiration: to live well in their place

The Cascadia Scorecard, a project started in 2004 by Sightline Institute, measures long-term progress in the Pacific Northwest. An index of seven trends shaping the future of the region, it is a simple but surprisingly far-reaching gauge. The Scorecard's indicators—health, economy, population, energy, sprawl, wildlife, and pollution—provide status reports for Cascadia and, by highlighting successful communities, offer a practical vision for a better Northwest.

Above all, the Scorecard puts a spotlight on the long view and the questions that most matter over great spans of time: Are we living longer, healthier lives? Are we building strong human communities? Are we handing down to our children a place whose economy is fair, and whose natural heritage is regenerating?

This 2007 edition of the Cascadia Scorecard is the fourth book in a series. The first book, *Cascadia Scorecard 2004*, presents a complete exposition of the seven trends: why they matter, what they mean, and what Cascadians can do about them. The second book, *Cascadia Scorecard 2005*, focused on the one Scorecard trend—energy—on which the region most lags behind world leaders. The third, *Cascadia Scorecard 2006*, concentrated on the interrelationship between two Scorecard trends, sprawl and health. This edition returns to examine progress on the Scorecard overall: Where has Cascadia made progress? Where have we fallen short? What are the implications of recent developments for our children's and grandchildren's prospects?

Cascadians who wish to learn more about the Scorecard and how to turn its indicators in the right direction can find and download ample additional information—including maps and charts in a number of formats; supplementary state-, provincial-, and local-level Scorecard data; and a version of this book with complete sources and citations—at *www.sightline.org*. While there, they can sign up for free electronic updates on the Scorecard by subscribing to one of our several email newsletters.

A NOTE ABOUT GEOGRAPHY

Cascadia's boundaries are natural, but data collection is typically delimited by political borders. Unless otherwise noted, references to Cascadia in the figures and charts in this book cover the entirety of Washington, Oregon, Idaho, and British Columbia, but not the adjoining portions of Alaska, Montana, California, or other neighboring states.

INTRODUCTION: WHAT PROGRESS?

CASCADIA SCORECARD

The Score: 43 years, on average, behind targets

The Trend: Improving slowly

The Story: Cascadia's Score—the region's average yearly performance on the seven Scorecard indicators—shows that the Northwest is making slow progress toward a healthy and lasting prosperity, but is still an average of 43 years away from meeting achievable, real-world goals. Cascadia's overall Score has been buoyed principally by improvements in life expectancy and smart growth. To accelerate progress, northwesterners can focus on energy efficiency, improving economic security for middle- and lower-income residents, and reducing stubbornly high rates of unintended pregnancies.

What if your bathroom scale has been wrong all along? Day after day, you step on, and take comfort—or sigh with disappointment—at the reading. But what if it's been telling you the poundage of some other person? Or, perhaps, the average of 30 strangers, picked seemingly at random? You might try to exchange your scale for one that works; or you might just toss it in the trash. Regardless, you'd certainly stop consulting it.

Now consider the Dow Jones industrial average. The Dow is the king of stock indicators—the bathroom scale of the global economy. When the media report on stocks, they treat other indicators—the S&P 500, the Russell 2000, and in Canada the T&S 2000—as color commentary. The Dow is the real story.

Since the mid-1980s, the Dow has risen tenfold, but middle-class incomes have scarcely budged

Yet the Dow is a lousy scale, the least meaningful of the major market indices. Its outdated methods serve as a reminder of the computational limits of the late nineteenth century: by simply averaging stock prices, while ignoring the number of shares of each stock in circulation, the Dow provides a distorted view of the market's ups and downs. Worse, its roster of 30 companies (out of more than 3,600 companies whose stocks are traded on the New York Stock Exchange, and perhaps ten times that number traded globally) is chosen without any particular methodology; two Dow Jones employees simply pick them. By now, with superior indices a mouse click away, using the Dow to gauge the market's mood is like using *The Old Farmer's Almanac* to predict the weather.

But through the power of repetition, our society has come to regard the Dow as a reliable scale not only for stock markets but for society's progress more generally. In the months preceding the November 2006 US election, for example, anxious politicians pointed to a strong economy—as evidenced by the record-breaking performance of the Dow—as cause for celebration.

Such claims were beyond chicanery; they were nonsense. For one thing, the Dow wasn't at record levels: adjusted for inflation, on Election Day it still stood 14 percentage points below its January 2000 peak. More importantly, the wealthiest fifth of Americans own 90 percent of all stock-market assets, while the bottom three-fifths of Americans own a scant 3 percent. The performance of the market, much less the Dow, has virtually no bearing on most people's pocketbooks. Since the mid-1980s the Dow has risen nearly tenfold, and real economic output in Cascadia has more than doubled. By comparison, middle-class incomes in the region scarcely budged (see Figure 1).

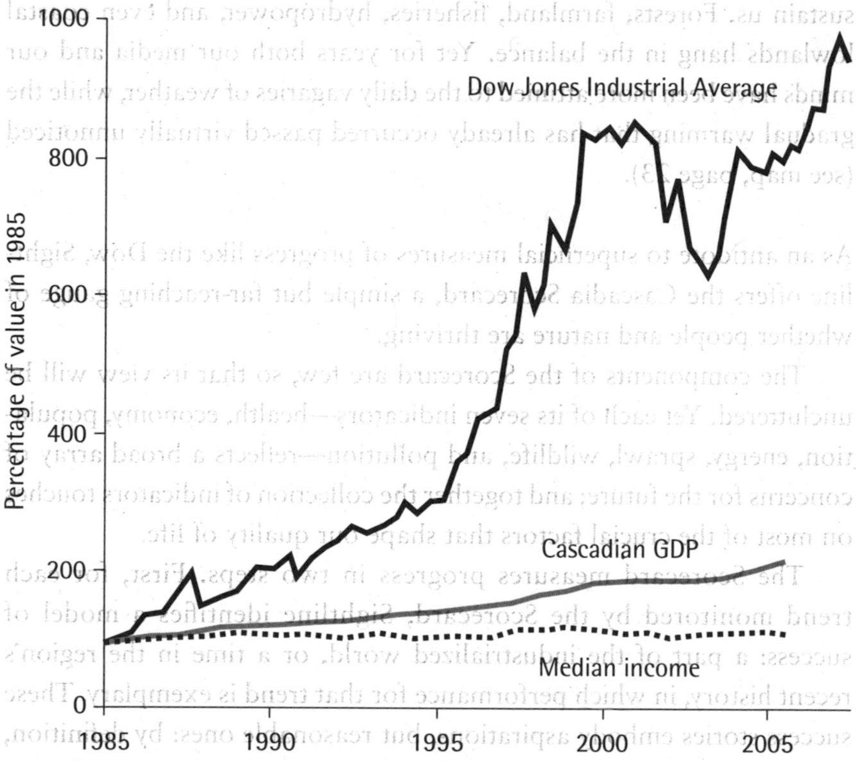

Figure 1.
Two decades of so-called progress: the Dow soared, Cascadia's economy doubled, but middle-class incomes barely budged.

The Dow, as misleading an indicator as it is, attracts attention in part because of convention. In a complicated world, the Dow is simple and familiar. It also attracts attention because it is mercurial. It can fluctuate widely from month to month, or even day to day. Psychologists and marketers have long known that our minds gravitate to the fast-changing, not the incremental—and this tendency may underlie our fascination with the ever-shifting Dow.

Cascadians' daily lives, however, are far more affected by trends that move with almost imperceptible slowness—trends for which we do not have reliable bathroom scales. For example, the gradual rise in atmospheric concentrations of greenhouse gases—resulting in part from our use of fossil fuels—threatens to wreak havoc on the landscapes that sustain us. Forests, farmland, fisheries, hydropower, and even coastal lowlands hang in the balance. Yet for years both our media and our minds have been more attuned to the daily vagaries of weather, while the gradual warming that has already occurred passed virtually unnoticed (see map, page 23).

As an antidote to superficial measures of progress like the Dow, Sightline offers the Cascadia Scorecard, a simple but far-reaching gauge of whether people and nature are thriving.

The components of the Scorecard are few, so that its view will be uncluttered. Yet each of its seven indicators—health, economy, population, energy, sprawl, wildlife, and pollution—reflects a broad array of concerns for the future; and together the collection of indicators touches on most of the crucial factors that shape our quality of life.

The Scorecard measures progress in two steps. First, for each trend monitored by the Scorecard, Sightline identifies a model of success: a part of the industrialized world, or a time in the region's recent history, in which performance for that trend is exemplary. These success stories embody aspirations, but reasonable ones: by definition, model performance is within reach, since it has already been achieved somewhere in the world. The Scorecard models do not necessarily represent the best possible performance on any indicator. Instead, they serve as wayposts, goals that—if reached—will put us well on track toward creating a healthy, lasting prosperity.

Second, Sightline calculates how many years it might take for Cascadia to catch up to the performance of the models. To do this, we calculate how much year-to-year change, whether good or bad, has been typical in recent decades. Sightline then determines how many years, at this rate of change, it would take to reach model performance, assuming the region makes progress every year and never backslides. Thus, each indicator's score, measured in "years to model performance," represents an optimistic estimate of how long it would take to reach real-world goals at the rate of change we are already used to. (We can likely achieve progress more quickly: the Scorecard isn't a prediction, just a uniform way to measure ourselves against our aspirations.) And the average of these scores is an overall measure of progress that is, while far from perfect, vastly superior to prevailing indicators such as the Dow.

By design, the Cascadia Scorecard provides a gauge of what matters, and of whether we're getting closer to achieving our shared goals. At the same time, the Scorecard provides a practical vision of what a prosperous and more sustainable place would look like—a place that combines elements of many real-world models of success.

Over the last two and a half decades, the Scorecard trends have not moved in lockstep. But the region's aggregate score has slowly climbed (see Figure 2), buoyed by steady gains in health and a gradual improvement, at least since the mid-1980s, in channeling growth into compact

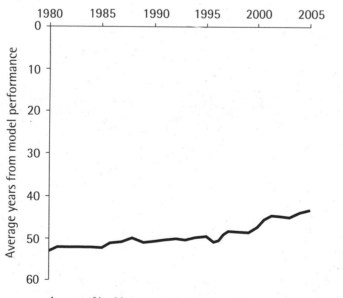

Average of health, economy, population, energy, sprawl, and wildlife

Figure 2.
The Cascadia Scorecard shows that our region has made slow but steady gains, with the average buoyed by improved health and smarter growth.

Key trend	Indicator	Target: Place with excellent— and achievable—record	Target
Health	Life expectancy at birth, in years	Japan, 2001	81.3 years
Economy	Composite index of unemployment rate, median income, and poverty rate, 1990 = 100	Selected high-performing states and provinces in recent years (European and wealthy Asian cities do better, but data not comparable.)	108.6 points
Population	Total fertility rate, in children born per woman	Netherlands and Sweden, 2001–02	1.7 births
Energy	Per capita use of highway fuel and nonindustrial electricity, in gallons of gasoline-equivalent per week	Germany, 2001	7.4 gallons
Sprawl	Percentage of metropolitan-area residents in compact, transit-friendly neighborhoods	Interim target: Vancouver, BC, 2001 (European and wealthy Asian cities do better, but data not comparable.)	62 percent
Wildlife	Populations of five key "indicator species," as a percentage of historic abundance	Interim target: one-third to one-half of levels prior to European arrival, depending on the species	43 percent
Pollution	Median concentration of toxic chemicals in breastmilk, in parts per billion	PBDEs: median levels in Japan, 2000 PCBs: lowest level found in Sightline study, 2004	1.3 parts per billion PBDEs, 51 parts per billion PCBs
Average:			

Table 1. Cascadia Scorecard 2007: The Northwest will require some 43 years of steady progress to meet ambitious but achievable goals.

Cascadia Scorecard 2007	Scorecard gap With steady progress, how many years to match target?	Status and trend
79.5 years	11 years	Would rank 12th best in world if an independent nation; improving slowly.
100.2 points	20 years	Strong by international standards. Improved for two consecutive years, but the region still trails the strong performance of the late 1990s.
1.8 births	12 years	Close to world's best, but variable; substantial progress since 1990, but worsened slightly over the last three years.
14.5 gallons	91 years	Worst performance among Scorecard trends; improved since 1999, but no net progress since 1990.
33 percent	57 years	Modest improvements in recent years are now threatened by new road building plans and new loopholes in growth laws. Region overall still lags far behind Vancouver, BC.
18 percent	69 years	Variable, though wolves are showing steady progress in recent years. In 2006, gains in wolf and salmon were offset by slight declines in orca and sage-grouse numbers.
50 parts per billion, PBDEs; 134 parts per billion, PCBs	? years (Time-series data unavailable.)	PBDEs among highest in world, concentrations likely rising. PCB levels apparently lower than national averages from previous decades, though precise comparisons are difficult.
	43 years	Improved fastest in late 1990s; slow improvements in the new millennium.

Compared with leaders from around the world, Cascadia lags behind

communities. In recent years, gains in key wildlife populations, especially wolves, have further boosted the Scorecard's performance, though continuations of those gains are now in doubt (see Wildlife indicator, page 41).

But compared with models from around the world, Cascadia lags an average of 43 years behind (see Table 1). At the recent pace of change, it would take 43 years of slow-and-steady progress to bring Cascadia's average performance up to the level that those places had already achieved when Sightline launched the Scorecard in 2004.

Meanwhile, the regions in the world that serve as models for the Scorecard are not standing still. They are racking up further improvements. Life expectancy in Japan, for example, increased by nearly a year between 2001 and 2004. Germany's consumption of highway fuels fell by about a tenth between 1999 and 2004—the rough equivalent of the entire country taking a one-month holiday from driving every year. More generally, Germans' net per capita consumption of highway fuels and nonindustrial electricity has fallen by one percent per year, while renewable energy generation in the country has averaged double-digit annual growth.

Progress on the Scorecard has been hampered most by the three trends that have been most resistant to change. Cascadia's energy consumption, fertility rates, and economic security are all at roughly the same levels in this year's Scorecard as they were in 1980. Focusing attention on those areas—particularly our overdependence on polluting sources of energy, which is both stubbornly high and furthest away from Scorecard models—would do the most to move Cascadia in the right direction.

1. HEALTH

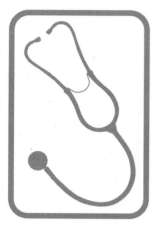

The Score: 11 years behind targets

The Trend: Improving steadily

The Story: Health, as measured by life expectancy, is the Scorecard's best-performing indicator. Lifespans now average 79.5 years in Cascadia, compared with 81.3 years for the Scorecard model. To accelerate progress, Cascadians can increase access to preventive medical care, design neighborhoods for safety and exercise, and improve the economic prospects of our neediest residents.

After surging in 2004, life expectancy in Cascadia improved only modestly in 2005, the most recent year for which regionwide data are available. Given prevailing patterns of mortality, a baby born in 2005 could expect 79 years and 6 months of life, up by about a month from the previous year (see Figure 3). That's one-fifth of the improvement logged in 2004, when average lifespans shot up by 7 months in Washington and 8 months in Idaho. But the trend is consistently positive. By the Scorecard's reckoning, Cascadia is only 11 years away from achieving the "model" performance chosen at the Scorecard's inception (Japan's life expectancy as of 2001), if we make steady progress each year.

Good health is important in its own right, and is also a sign that other aspects of our lives are going well. If our air and water grow more polluted, our lives more stressful, our society more dangerous, or

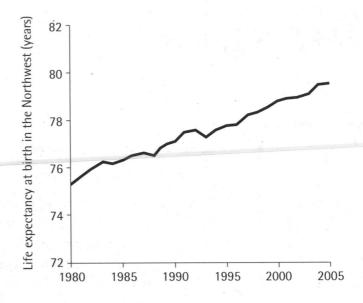

Figure 3.
Cascadians, on
average, are living
more than four
years longer than
they were in 1980.

our economy less able to meet our needs, then our health is likely to deteriorate as well.

The Cascadia Scorecard measures health through life expectancy, probably the globe's most common yardstick of population health. Technically, life expectancy is the average number of years a newborn can expect to live, given current patterns of mortality. It is a reliable health gauge because it integrates all maladies that can shorten lives, from infant mortality to heart disease to traffic accidents to cancer. Moreover, national and international comparisons show striking correlations between life expectancy and other measures of health, such as the number of years people live free of disability and even people's satisfaction with their own health.

Life expectancy has grown slowly but steadily for decades in Cascadia. At the dawn of the twentieth century, a resident of the region could expect to reach the age of about 50. But 100 years later, average lifespans had stretched to nearly 79 years: more growth in a single century than in all of prior human history. And the growth of life expectancy shows little sign of abating: over the most recent decade, average lifespans increased by nearly 2 years, as the toll from virtually every major cause of death declined.

Gains in health have been uneven, however. British Columbia remains far and away the healthiest jurisdiction in Cascadia. Provincial residents can expect 81.1 years of life—topping all other North American states and provinces. In fact, if British Columbia were an independent nation, it would rank second in the world in life expectancy, trailing only Japan. If recent trends continue, the province may match or exceed the Scorecard model within two years.

Within British Columbia, the healthiest areas are in the south (see map, page 24.) The healthiest jurisdiction in British Columbia, and Cascadia overall, is the suburban city of Richmond, where lifespans exceed 83 years—higher than Japan's, and also higher than those of any major county in the United States. Jurisdictions within the Northwest states don't fare as well. The Northwest counties with the longest lifespans, Washington County, Oregon, and King County, Washington, aren't even standouts among populous US counties. To look for leadership in improving health, residents of the Northwest states should cast their gaze northward.

British Columbians' success in leading long, healthy lives is the result not of one cause but of many. While the province's health care system certainly has its detractors, none of its inhabitants goes without health insurance—unlike the 1 in 7 residents of the Northwest states who go without such insurance each year. British Columbia also has lower rates of violent deaths: fewer homicides and also fewer fatal car crashes, the latter largely due to compact communities that allow residents to drive less than their neighbors to the south. Even economics may play a role. On average, residents of the province aren't as wealthy as their American counterparts, but the income and wealth gaps between the rich and the poor are narrower. Around the world, an unequal economic structure tends to be associated with poor health. Other factors—including lower

British Columbians' success in leading long, healthy lives is the result not of one cause but of many

rates of severe obesity, compared with the Northwest states—may also play a role in the province's exceptional record.

In the Northwest states, improving access to preventive medical care—as Washington did in 2007 for lower-income children—could be a boon to lifespans. But medical care is only part of the solution to better health. Just as important are more systemic changes that keep us healthy without medical intervention. Redesigning our neighborhoods so that we can walk more and drive less, for example, would help promote regular exercise while limiting deaths and injuries from car crashes. Similarly, taking steps to reduce poverty could alleviate economic and social strains that contribute to poor health.

2. ECONOMY

The Score: 20 years behind targets

The Trend: No progress

The Story: Combining trends in median income, poverty, child poverty, and unemployment, the Cascadia Scorecard shows that economic security has made meager gains in the Northwest states since 1990, and has actually declined in British Columbia. As a first step toward improving this score, Cascadian jurisdictions need an accurate gauge of middle- and lower-income well-being. Without that, Cascadia is flying blind.

Between 1990 and 2005, the Northwest's combined economic output—its gross regional product—grew by 72 percent, after adjusting for inflation, while total personal income rose by an inflation-adjusted 56 percent. But these oft-noted measures of the Northwest's economy can be deceptive. The seeming good news masks a less encouraging story. The most recent data on economic security shows that middle- and lower-income people in Cascadia have made virtually no progress in 15 years (see Figure 4).

Average income fails as a measure of economic well-being because it doesn't distinguish between the wealthy (whose incomes have risen handsomely in recent years) and everyone else (whose economic prospects aren't nearly so rosy). To provide a more complete picture of the Northwest's progress toward fair markets and broadly shared

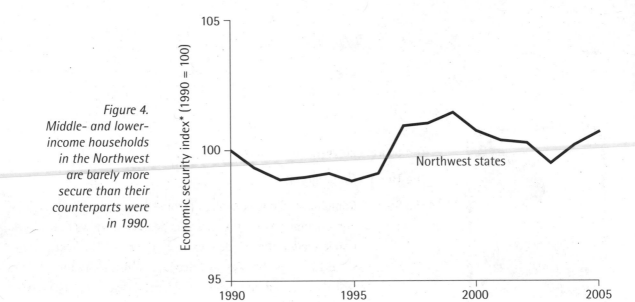

Figure 4. Middle- and lower-income households in the Northwest are barely more secure than their counterparts were in 1990.

* The economic security index is compiled from median income, unemployment, poverty, and child poverty.

prosperity—especially for the region's middle- and lower-income residents—the Scorecard employs a four-part gauge of economic security combining unemployment rates, median incomes, poverty rates, and the share of children living below the poverty line. Nationally, these measures tend to move together; when unemployment goes down, poverty and child poverty tend to fall and median income to rise. By combining these trends, the Scorecard provides a fuller picture of economic security than one trend alone can offer.

The Scorecard looks to high-performing regions of the US and Canada as models. (Other nations may have substantially better performance, but the data aren't comparable.) For the US Northwest, the models are the Upper Midwest states of Iowa, Minnesota, and Wisconsin, which are similar in population to the Northwest states, and which enjoyed robust middle-class incomes and low rates of unemployment and poverty when the Scorecard was created in 2004. For British Columbia (which uses a slightly different measure of poverty than does the US), the prairie provinces of Alberta, Manitoba, and Saskatchewan serve as the model.

The Scorecard reveals that, despite a few small improvements, many middle- and lower-income northwesterners still face precarious economic conditions. After years of ups and downs, by 2005 the poverty rate remained unchanged from 1990, while the child poverty rate was slightly lower and the unemployment rate slightly higher.

The Scorecard does show evidence of some recent gains, however: economic security in 2005 was a bit better than it was in 2004, which in turn was better than 2003. These gains were driven by declining rates of unemployment and poverty. Median income, however, has been a mixed bag for the Northwest states. After adjusting for inflation, median income is higher today than it was in 1990, yet it remains several thousand dollars below its 1998 peak.

Relative to its performance in 1990, British Columbia has fared no better than the Northwest states. In 2004, the last year for which complete data are available, the province had a substantially larger percentage of its residents below the low-income cutoff (sometimes referred to as the Canadian poverty line) than it did in 1990. Its percentage of children living in families below the low-income cutoff has also grown. British Columbians' overall economic security is worse than it was in 1990 (see Figure 5).

Like residents of the Northwest states, however, British Columbians have seen their economic security improve recently. In 2004, the province mirrored national Canadian trends and realized a second consecutive year of progress. The bright spot in British Columbia's economic performance was its unemployment rate, which continued to decline from the much higher levels of the early 1990s. Median income also improved in 2004, yet remains about 6 percent lower than it was in 1990.

The figures that make up the Scorecard's economy indicator are the most complete and up-to-date available. Yet the figures for poverty and child

Policymakers have little information about the financial security of working families

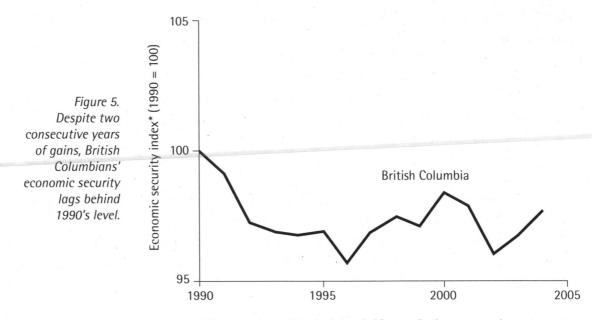

Figure 5.
Despite two
consecutive years
of gains, British
Columbians'
economic security
lags behind
1990's level.

* The economic security index is compiled from median income, unemployment, poverty, and child poverty.

poverty in British Columbia are already nearly three years old. Data for the Northwest states are only slightly better; figures for 2005 were made available to the public late in 2006. Moreover, the margins of error for state and provincial estimates of income and poverty are so wide that it's often difficult to tell if economic conditions for the poor and middle class are improving, deteriorating, or simply stagnating.

For all the attention that we give to our pocketbooks in our personal lives, policymakers have little information about the financial security of working families. Yet without an accurate gauge of economic security, Cascadia's leaders are flying blind, with only a rudimentary compass to guide them. So while many innovative reforms could help boost Cascadians' financial well-being, it will be impossible to know if they're working until there is a reliable, regularly updated gauge of the financial health of ordinary working families.

3. POPULATION

The Score: 12 years behind targets

The Trend: Recent uptick, but little change overall from the early 1980s

The Story: Despite a small increase in the last two years, fertility rates in Cascadia have held stable for decades. The region's fertility patterns—which are both signals of women's status and harbingers of environmental impact—are close to the international models of Sweden and the Netherlands, where women's and children's well-being is high. To make progress on this indicator, Cascadians can reduce the stubbornly high rates of births from unintended pregnancies, particularly in the Northwest states.

Since the peak of the baby boom in the late 1950s, Cascadians have gradually shifted their patterns of childbearing toward smaller families that come later in life. In 2005, the last year for which complete data are available, average family size remained essentially stable at 1.8 children, a level that had changed only modestly over the previous two and a half decades (see Figure 6).

A growing population may seem a sign of prosperity, but in at least three ways, the opposite is more likely the case. First, poverty leads to larger families and prosperity yields smaller ones: the world's wealthy nations tend to have far lower rates of population growth than do struggling ones. Second, rapid population growth—to which birthrates can be a

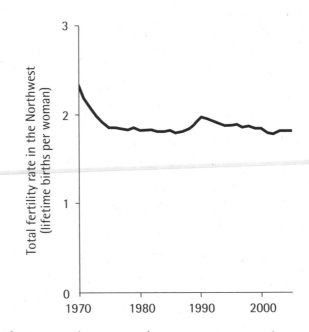

Figure 6.
Cascadian fertility
rates have stabilized
at just under two
births per woman.

significant contributor—tends to put a greater strain on a region's natural systems, from open space to water supply to air quality.

Finally, average family size (lifetime births per woman or, more precisely, the "total fertility rate") is an excellent gauge of women's, and families', well-being. It tends to decline when women have more control over important life decisions, better access to techniques for pregnancy prevention, and more economic and educational opportunities. Take, for example, Sweden and the Netherlands, the models for the Scorecard's population indicator. Both nations rank atop international comparisons of the well-being of women and children. Both societies offer generous support for families with young children. Both have few teen births and few births resulting from undesired pregnancies. And in both places, the fertility rate hovers around 1.7 lifetime births per woman.

In 1970, women in both British Columbia and the Northwest states were having an average of about 2.4 children each over the course of their lives. In the subsequent 35 years, the US and Canadian portions of the region have pulled apart. Women in British Columbia have reduced their average family size to just 1.4 children, while in the Northwest states women have held their families fairly stable at about 2 children each (see Figure 7). The disparities are even larger between different Cascadian districts (see map, page 25). In Canyon County, Idaho, and Yakima County, Washington, women average 2.7 births over their lifetimes. Cascadia's largest cities, by contrast, have smaller families: women in Vancouver, British Columbia, average about one child each; in Victoria and its environs, the average rises to 1.3; in the Eugene area, 1.5; and 1.7 is the norm in the counties that comprise Seattle and Portland. Farther out from these big cities and in greater Spokane and Boise, the average rises to about 2 children.

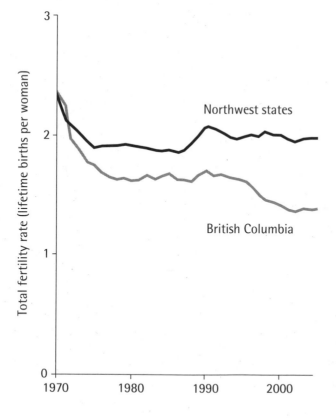

Figure 7.
Fertility patterns in
British Columbia and
the Northwest states
are diverging.

Births among young women declined more slowly in 2005 than in other recent years. For the third year running, teen birthrates set a record low, though they declined less than in any year of the last decade (see Figure 8). All parts of the region except Oregon contributed to this decrease and, as in prior years, British Columbia led the way. Today, the province's teen birthrates are one-third the average for the Northwest states. Births among women in their early twenties are also diminishing throughout Cascadia, while births among women in their thirties and forties are slowly rising.

Cascadia's shift toward smaller, later families is far from complete. Teen births in the Northwest states are twice as common as in the Netherlands. Moreover, more than one-third of all births (as well as

Figure 8.
Teen births have fallen
rapidly, especially in
British Columbia.

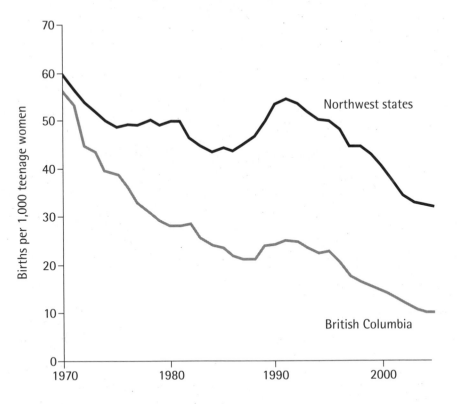

virtually all abortions) in the Northwest states stem from unintended pregnancies—those that are earlier than desired or not desired at all.

Preventing unintended pregnancies is a critical goal. It's one that can unite Cascadians with diverse values, because prevention brings compounding benefits: it prevents abortions and it leads to healthier children. Children conceived intentionally receive better prenatal care and are less likely to have dangerously low weights at birth or to die in infancy. They display superior verbal development in their early years and are less likely to endure abuse and neglect. Consequently, fewer wanted children end up in the child welfare system, including juvenile courts and foster care. Lowering unwanted pregnancies also slows population growth. For all these reasons, Cascadians' population goal should be for every child to be born wanted.

Thus, it's worrisome that the region's overall rate of unintended births has diminished little in the past decade. The stubborn stability of unintended births, even as numbers of births to teens and women in their early twenties have plummeted, is both puzzling and disappointing.

One likely explanation came to light in a Guttmacher Institute study in mid-2006. Nationwide US data show that, at least from 1994 to 2001, unintended pregnancy rates jumped 29 percent among poor women, as their access to publicly supported family-planning services and private medical insurance shrank. Meanwhile, unintended pregnancy rates dropped 20 percent among middle- and upper-class women. Apparently, unintended pregnancies have become increasingly bifurcated by class.

No one knows whether this national trend explains Cascadia's slowing progress and unchanging rate of unintended births. Through periodic surveys of new mothers, the Northwest states have begun measuring what matters about population—whether we're making progress toward a Northwest where every child is born wanted. But the surveys are too small to detect trends among women of different classes and backgrounds. Better measurement could guide our next steps.

Preventing unintended pregnancies is a critical goal

British Columbia's phenomenal success in reducing teen births and enabling women to choose smaller families later in life suggests that the province is doing many things right. Public policies in Canada have helped yield lower rates of poverty and inequality than in the Northwest states; in addition, comprehensive access to medical care, including reproductive-health care, and ready access to contraception and abortion services without stigma have likely contributed to British Columbia's more-rapid progress toward small, planned families.

Cascadia's progress toward smaller, planned families that come along later in life may have slowed, but two recent victories could help speed it up again. First, in April 2006 Montana joined Washington and California among Cascadian states that mandate equal treatment of prescription contraceptives in prescription-drug plans. Oregon's legislature was considering a bill to do the same as of early 2007. Insurance coverage for prescription contraceptives increases the percentage of couples who use the most effective forms of contraception, such as the pill. Enacting similar rules throughout Cascadia would prevent hundreds of unplanned pregnancies each year, helping to stem both births and abortions.

Second, in August 2006, after much delay, the US Food and Drug Administration followed Canada's example and approved nonprescription distribution of emergency contraceptive pills to adult women. This change will help tens of thousands of couples in the Northwest make sure that all their children are born wanted. It will help prevent both unintended pregnancies and unwelcome abortions. Unfortunately, the FDA did not extend emergency contraceptive access to minors, despite the fact that the median age of first intercourse for American women is 17.5 years. More than half of American women are sexually active before their eighteenth birthdays, but—for now—these young women need a doctor's prescription to buy emergency contraception.

ESTIMATED TEMPERATURE
INCREASE IN DEGREES F, 1950–2003

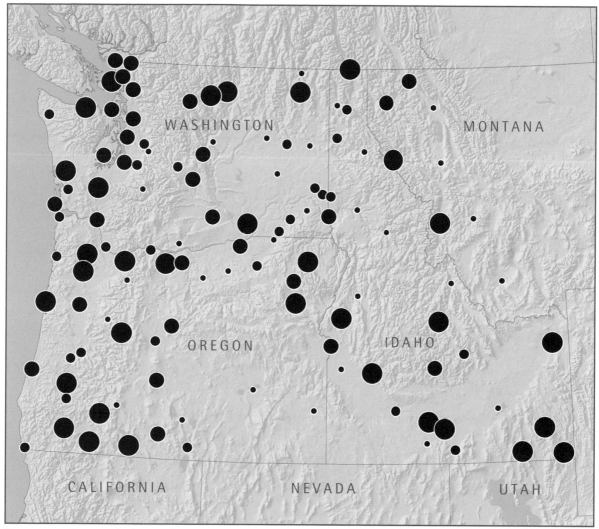

Temperature increase in degrees F, 1950–2003

- •   < 1.25
- ●   1.25–1.74
- ●   1.75–2.24
- ●   ≥ 2.25

Weather stations throughout the Northwest states show evidence of a long-term warming trend. Source: US Historical Climate Network, processed by Philip Mote, Washington State Climatologist. Data represent the best linear fit for average annual surface air temperature trends at each monitoring station. Map by CORE GIS.

LIFE EXPECTANCY AT BIRTH, 1999–2003

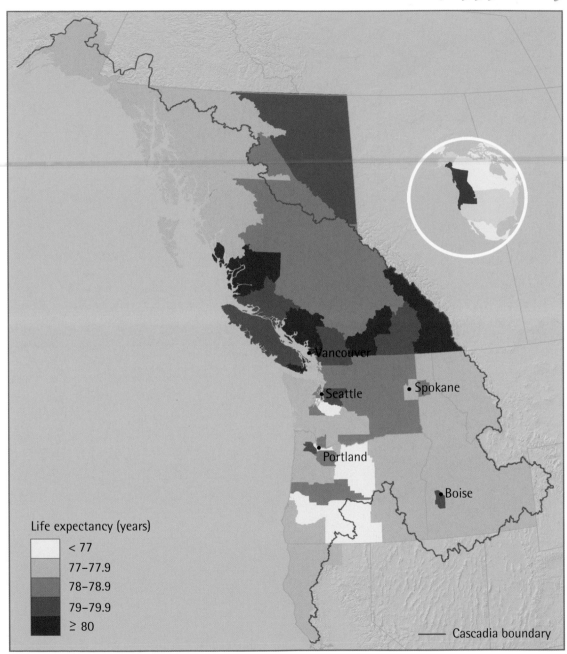

Life expectancy (years)

- < 77
- 77–77.9
- 78–78.9
- 79–79.9
- ≥ 80

—— Cascadia boundary

Residents of southern British Columbia have the longest average lifespans of any Cascadians.
Map by CommEn Space.

TOTAL FERTILITY RATE
(AVERAGE LIFETIME BIRTHS PER WOMAN), 2004

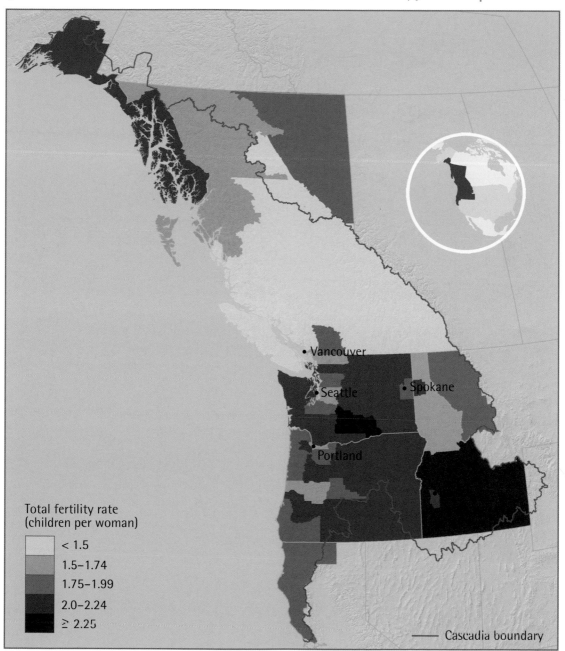

Total fertility rate
(children per woman)

- \< 1.5
- 1.5–1.74
- 1.75–1.99
- 2.0–2.24
- ≥ 2.25

—— Cascadia boundary

Southern Idaho has Cascadia's largest families on average, while southern British Columbia has the smallest. Map by CommEn Space.

NEW RESIDENTS IN LOW-DENSITY
SUBURBS AND EXURBS, 1990–2000

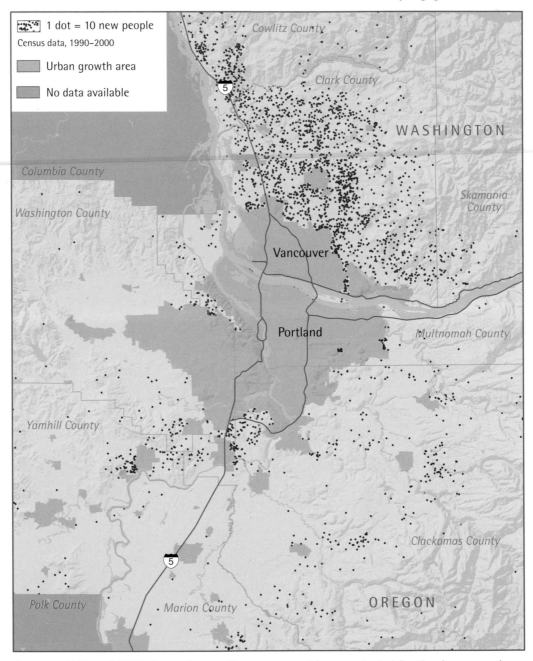

1 dot = 10 new people
Census data, 1990–2000

Urban growth area

No data available

Between 1990 and 2000, Oregon's growth management laws protected Portland-area rural open space from poorly planned sprawl, especially when compared with Clark County, Washington. Map by CommEn Space and CORE GIS.

ESTIMATED POPULATION GROWTH IN RURAL AREAS RESULTING FROM MEASURE 37 CLAIMS, 2004–2006

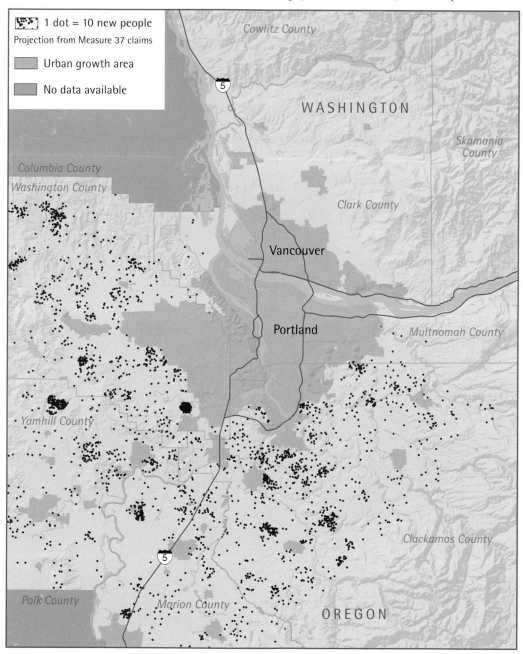

1 dot = 10 new people
Projection from Measure 37 claims

Urban growth area

No data available

Measure 37 has set the stage for poorly planned sprawl in the farms and rural areas surrounding Portland. Map by CORE GIS.

MORE MAPS, GRAPHICS, AND DATA AT SIGHTLINE.ORG

You can access animated versions of maps on our website at www.sightline.org. You'll also find print and web versions of Scorecard maps and charts for your use; and supplementary state, provincial, and local Scorecard data.

4. ENERGY

The Score: 91 years behind targets

The Trend: Stuck in high gear

The Story: Energy is the worst-performing indicator on the Scorecard. Counting highway fuels and electricity in homes and businesses, Cascadians consume the energy-equivalent of 2.1 gallons of gasoline every day—nearly double the Scorecard model, Germany. To improve this trend, Cascadians can increase efficiency in cars, lighting, and appliances, and accelerate the growth of transit- and pedestrian-friendly neighborhoods.

The Scorecard's energy indicator—the per capita consumption of motor fuels by cars and trucks and the use of electricity in homes and commercial buildings—reveals a region every bit as profligate with energy today as it was three decades ago (see Figure 9). In a typical week in 2006, Cascadians burned an average of 7.2 gallons of gasoline per capita in cars, SUVs, and minivans; consumed 2.3 gallons of diesel fuel, mostly for trucks; and used enough electricity in homes and businesses to keep 10 one-hundred-watt light bulbs burning continuously. Compared with the citizens of Germany, the model for the Scorecard's energy indicator, Cascadians are energy gluttons, and we have done nothing in recent years to trim our appetites.

But the flat line for overall energy use conceals three diverging trends. Gasoline consumption, measured per person, has been falling for seven years—a reduction that has taken place virtually unnoticed by media

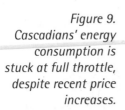

*Figure 9.
Cascadians' energy
consumption is
stuck at full throttle,
despite recent price
increases.*

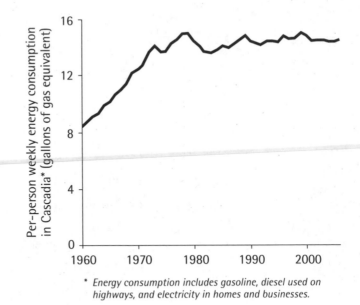

* *Energy consumption includes gasoline, diesel used on
highways, and electricity in homes and businesses.*

and policymakers alike. Meanwhile, electricity use jumped up last year, reversing several years of tentative progress toward greater efficiency, while the use of diesel fuel continued a slow, half-century-long ascent.

Abundant energy makes our lives much easier than they were in the not-so-distant days when the most reliable energy sources were firewood and muscle power. But many of the region's most serious problems are tied to high rates of energy use. Each barrel of oil we burn for highway fuels, for example, adds nearly half a ton of climate-warming gases to the atmosphere; releases perhaps 60 pounds of carbon monoxide, soot, and smog-forming compounds that endanger our health; siphons between $50 and $70 out of the local economy; increases the risk of oil spills and pipeline leaks; and entangles our region with some of the most volatile and politically unstable regimes in the world. Cascadians consume more than 300 million of those barrels each year. Coal and natural gas carry many of the same or similar costs, and hydropower dams cut salmon off from vast areas of spawning habitat.

As a proxy for Cascadia's overall energy consumption, the Scorecard tracks the per-person consumption of highway fuels and electricity in homes and buildings. These commodities are closely monitored and reliably updated, and over the last several decades they have closely mirrored trends in total energy consumption in the region. Germany, the model for Scorecard trends, enjoys high standards of living while consuming far less energy per person than the Northwest does. Moreover, that nation has aggressively pursued efficiency and renewable energy policies in recent years. While Germany still emits far more than its share of global-warming emissions from fossil fuels, it nevertheless stands as a developed-world model that Cascadia can aspire to match.

Rising costs at the pump have subtly changed our driving habits

Total gasoline consumption in Cascadia has remained flat since 1999, even as the region's population has grown by 9 percent. In the Northwest states, these two trends have combined to reduce per capita gasoline consumption to its lowest level since 1967. The drop has been steepest in Idaho: Cascadia's most rural jurisdiction still has the region's highest per capita gas consumption, at 8.4 gallons per person per week, but this is down by almost a gallon a week since 1999. Despite these reductions, though, residents of the Northwest states still use about 55 percent more gasoline per person than their counterparts in British Columbia (see Figure 10).

High gas prices are likely at the root of declining per-person consumption. In the late 1990s, a gallon of gasoline was as cheap as it had ever been, adjusted for inflation. But since then, prices have risen by about 10 percent a year, and natural-gas prices have risen even more quickly. Annual spending to import crude oil and natural gas into the Northwest states has tripled in less than a decade (see Figure 11), and topped $19 billion in 2006.

Rising costs at the pump have created financial strains, but they have also subtly changed our driving habits. Transportation analysts say that rising gasoline prices in recent years have boosted transit ridership and

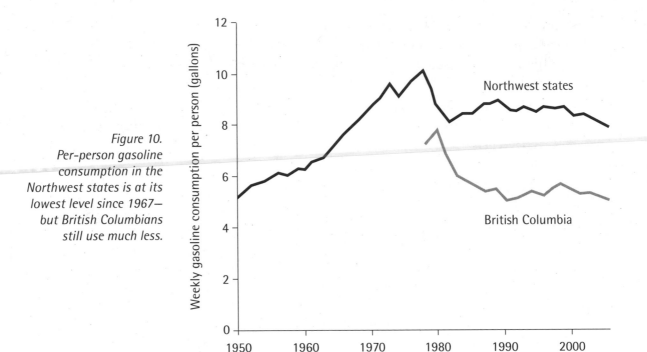

Figure 10.
Per-person gasoline
consumption in the
Northwest states is at its
lowest level since 1967—
but British Columbians
still use much less.

sales of fuel-efficient vehicles, while dampening sales of the most wasteful gas-guzzlers. For families with more than one vehicle, high prices have encouraged the use of the one with better gas mileage. Rising gas costs may even be reducing northwesterners' appetite for car travel, by encouraging drivers to plan shorter trips and to combine several errands into a single outing. According to the Federal Highway Administration, the total number of miles logged on the roads in Oregon and Washington decreased from 2004 to 2005—an unusual decline at a time when overall economic activity expanded. Combined, Cascadians' steps toward fuel efficiency have paid off, reducing overall spending on gasoline in the region by as much as $1.3 billion in 2006.

The price of diesel fuel has increased in tandem with that of gasoline. But unlike gasoline use, per capita diesel use is still on the upswing: annual consumption was just under 100 gallons per person a decade ago,

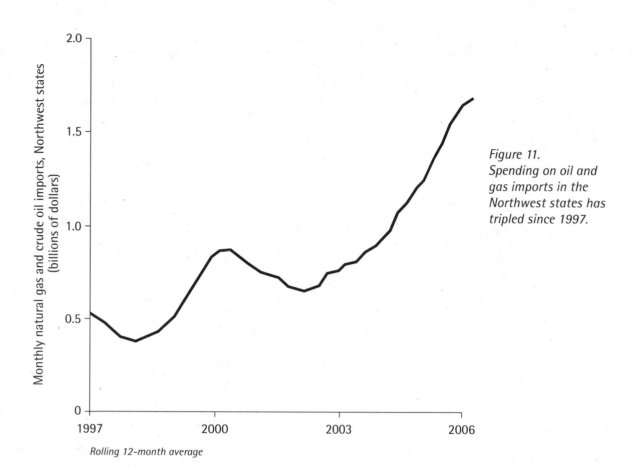

Figure 11.
Spending on oil and
gas imports in the
Northwest states has
tripled since 1997.

Rolling 12-month average

but it rose to 119 gallons last year. Most of the region's diesel goes into the fuel tanks of heavy trucks used for long-distance hauling. For decades, the globalization of manufacturing and farming has increased the distance between consumers and producers, which in turn has steadily increased freight transportation and thus per capita diesel use. Apparently, recent increases in diesel prices have done little to dampen this trend.

Perhaps the biggest source of concern in the Scorecard's energy indicator is the recent rise in electricity consumption. Electricity prices climbed rapidly from 2000 through 2002, the consequence of an electricity crisis that swept outward from California. Higher prices

The recent sea change in Cascadia's global-warming policies is likely to yield huge benefits for energy efficiency

quelled consumption, but only temporarily: between 2003 and 2006, total electricity consumption by Cascadia's homes and businesses rebounded, rising by roughly 7 percent. Meanwhile, imports of coal to produce electric power have grown. In December 2006, Washington's Centralia coal mine closed for good; the nearby twin coal-fired power plants—by far the largest source of greenhouse gas emissions in Cascadia—now import their coal from Wyoming's Powder River Basin. As a result, the Northwest states now import virtually all the fossil fuels used to produce electricity.

Encouragingly, Cascadian jurisdictions are beginning to seize opportunities to reduce the impacts, both economic and environmental, of its energy consumption. The recent sea change in global-warming policies throughout Cascadia, for example, is likely to yield huge benefits for energy efficiency. California took the lead, by curbing coal-fired power plants and setting the stage for a comprehensive cap-and-trade system for reducing the state's carbon emissions. British Columbia followed suit, with an even more ambitious program designed to dovetail with California's. Oregon and Washington are considering similar steps. All these policies have the potential to ramp up the production of renewable energy, while focusing attention on the cheapest opportunities to reduce carbon emissions and energy waste throughout the region.

A critical next step in accelerating such progress is to make energy prices tell the truth. After all, as expensive as a gallon of gasoline may seem, the price still fails to cover the costs of global warming, air pollution, and petroleum-related military spending. In fact, taxes paid by drivers don't even pay for all the costs of roads. As recent trends show, Cascadians are sensitive to gasoline prices and can find ways to trim wasteful consumption when given the right incentives. Ensuring that all consumers pay the full cost of their energy purchases—rather than pushing those costs onto their neighbors or their grandchildren—can help create an economy that is simultaneously more efficient and more fair.

5. SPRAWL

The Score: 57 years behind targets

The Trend: Slow improvement

The Story: Low-density sprawl is still the norm in Cascadia's cities, but compact communities are staging a resurgence, with the share of residents living in walkable or transit-oriented neighborhoods increasing in each major metropolis. Still, given recent trends, it will take 57 years for the Cascadian city average to match what Vancouver, BC, has already achieved. The keys to combating sprawl are protecting farmland, promoting infill development, and limiting sprawl-inducing road projects.

Since at least World War II, sprawl—dispersed, poorly planned, car-centered development that segregates homes from stores and jobs—has been the dominant form of residential development in North America. In past editions of the Cascadia Scorecard, Sightline analyzed and mapped sprawl in the Northwest's 7 largest cities, as well as in 12 additional cities across the United States. These analyses showed that as major Northwest cities grow in population, they are also making gradual progress in channeling new growth into compact, transit- and pedestrian-oriented neighborhoods (see Figure 12). Vancouver, British Columbia, stands out as having the best smart-growth record among all the cities Sightline has studied (see Figure 13), and it stands as the Scorecard's model for success. At present rates of change, it will take 57 years for Cascadia's cities, on average, to match Vancouver's record as of 2001.

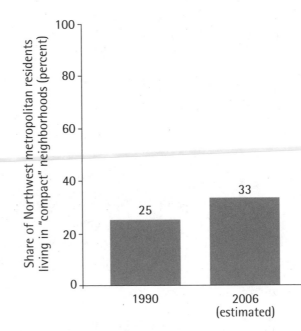

Figure 12.
Cascadia's major cities
are gradually channeling
more of their growth into
compact neighborhoods.

Sprawl contributes to a panoply of ills. It confines residents in cars for virtually every trip, increases transportation and infrastructure costs, frays forests, harms streams and wildlife, overruns farmland, and commits the region to exorbitant expenditures on roads, vehicles, and highway fuels. It can even undermine health by limiting exercise and increasing automotive collisions, as the 2006 edition of the Scorecard detailed.

The Scorecard measures sprawl by the share of residents who live in neighborhoods compact enough to allow bus transit and walking as alternatives to the car. The sprawl record of greater Vancouver, BC, is far from perfect: new job growth, for example, often takes place far from new housing. Nonetheless, it has the most compact urban structure of any of the 19 cities Sightline has analyzed to date. Vancouver's development trends stand out both for protecting open space and for channeling new residents into compact neighborhoods.

But among US jurisdictions, Portland, Oregon, has stood out favorably in past editions of the Scorecard, particularly for preserving

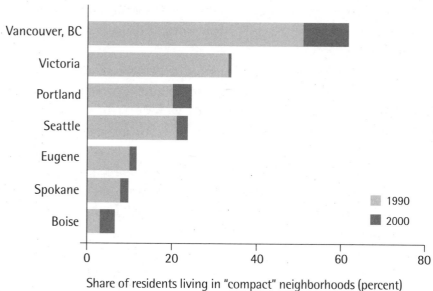

Figure 13.
Among all Cascadian
cities, Vancouver leads
the way in smart growth.

farmland and protecting open space on the urban fringe. Oregon's success could be traced to its statewide land-use policies, which were designed to keep farmland intact by channeling growth into designated urban and suburban areas. In 2007, however, Oregon's smart-growth leadership appears to be coming to an end.

This decline is the result of Measure 37, a "pay-or-waive" law that Oregon voters approved by a wide margin in 2004. In essence, pay-or-waive laws force taxpayers to offer compensation when communities' rules restrict what property owners can do on their land. Ordinary zoning, urban growth boundaries, and watershed protections can all trigger compensation. If taxpayers cannot pay, as is almost always the case, then property owners are entitled to a waiver from the restriction.

In the roughly two years that Oregon has lived under Measure 37, landowners have filed some 7,000 claims requesting many billions of dollars of compensation. In the Portland metro region alone, claimants filed more than 2,000 residential applications for Measure 37 waivers.

Together, these claims could add nearly 14,000 housing units and 36,000 new residents, mostly on the urban fringe outside of agreed-upon growth boundaries.

These new Measure 37 claims are a sharp contrast to greater Portland's previous successes at containing sprawl, which are notable. When one compares the Portland area with adjacent Clark County, Washington, for example, it's clear that Oregon's growth management laws helped constrain low-density development at the outskirts of metropolitan Portland during the 1990s (see map, page 26). Part of this difference is due to the fact that Washington's urban-growth regulations did not take effect until the second half of the decade. Still, the comparison clearly showed that Oregon's growth policies served as a brake on sprawl.

Measure 37 claims are a sharp contrast to greater Portland's previous successes at containing sprawl

Unfortunately, in just two years Measure 37 has unleashed claims holding the potential for nearly as much low-density, exurban sprawl as Clark County, Washington, endured in the entire decade of the 1990s (see map, page 27).

Oregon's experiment with Measure 37 blazed the trail for others. In 2006, a national anti-planning movement seized on Measure 37's victory at the ballot box and pushed copycat initiatives in six Western states including California, Idaho, and Washington. Fortunately, voters in these neighboring states soundly rejected pay-or-waive laws.

Ironically, just as Oregon's neighbors were rejecting pay-or-waive, the effects of Measure 37 got even more extreme. In the two weeks that preceded an administrative deadline in November 2006, Oregon jurisdictions received a barrage of Measure 37 claims, doubling the total number of exemptions requested. The last-minute claims included the biggest one so far: an out-of-state logging corporation, Plum Creek Timber, filed nearly 100 applications to allow development on 32,000 acres of coastal forest. Plum Creek demanded $95 million in compensation from taxpayers unless it is allowed to build on the land, most of which is zoned for forestry.

By early 2007, a backlash against Measure 37 was mounting, as Oregon residents discovered that Measure 37 provides less choice than it appears to. Communities have neither the resources to contest the Measure 37 claims filed against them nor the cash to pay the claims. So communities are forced to waive the property restrictions instead. As a result, Measure 37 may be undermining the very rights it claimed to protect: many Oregonians are losing their ability to protect their own properties from bad neighbors.

By rejecting pay-or-waive laws, the other Northwest states reaffirmed the importance of land-use planning and local decision-making. Planning is a tough and contentious process, like so much of democracy, and is certain to remain so. But it is vastly preferable to the alternative: unplanned, wasteful sprawl.

6. WILDLIFE

The Score: 69 years behind targets

The Trend: Modest gains, led by wolves and salmon

The Story: The five representative Cascadian wildlife populations tracked by the Scorecard are all far below their historic abundance. Wolves have staged a remarkable comeback in Montana and Idaho in recent years, while sage-grouse and chinook salmon have improved modestly. But orcas and Selkirk caribou have struggled. To move these species off life support, Cascadians can work to restore the natural landscapes and ecosystems on which they depend.

The 2007 Scorecard shows modest gains in wildlife numbers in recent years (see Figure 14). The improvements were led by a recovery of wolf populations in Idaho and Montana, and to a lesser extent by several years of relatively abundant chinook runs. Still, so diminished are these species from their historical levels that, at current rates of progress, it would take 69 years to restore these populations to Scorecard targets—which themselves represent just a fraction of these species' original abundance.

For the region's first human inhabitants, Cascadia was defined by its wildlife. The spectacularly abundant salmon played a central role in First Nations cultures, while orcas, wolves, and countless other species populated tribal myths. Even today, with their abundance severely

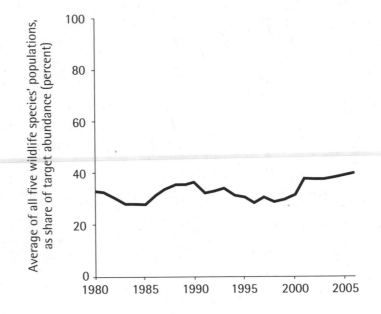

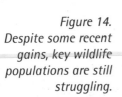

Figure 14. Despite some recent gains, key wildlife populations are still struggling.

reduced, Cascadia's native species remain not only a source of wonder and fascination, but also an economic engine for tourism, fisheries, and other industries (see Figure 15). Just as important, the abundance of the region's wildlife offers insights into the health of the natural ecosystems that support and enrich our lives.

The Cascadia Scorecard's wildlife indicator tracks five key wildlife populations: gray wolves in Idaho and Montana; the Selkirk herd of mountain caribou; Oregon's greater sage-grouse; the southern resident orcas of Puget Sound and the Strait of Georgia; and the chinook salmon that return in the spring and summer to the Columbia River. In the Scorecard, these species serve as proxies for the natural wealth that northwesterners have inherited and for our stewardship of that inheritance. If the region's forests, deserts, rivers, and marine waters are healthy and thriving, then Cascadia's salmon, orcas, wolves, caribou, and sage-grouse will thrive too. If not, these creatures will dwindle and disappear.

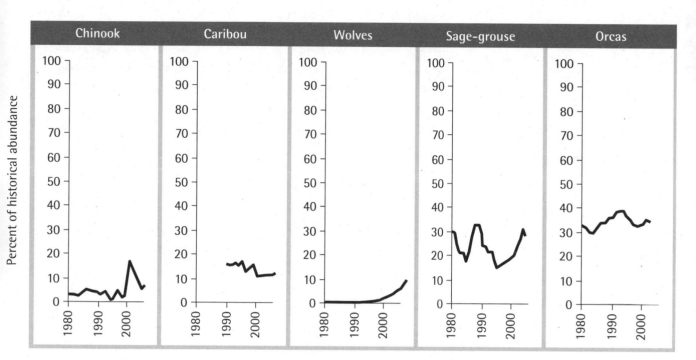

The models for the wildlife indicator represent modest targets: restoring key wildlife populations to one-third or one-half of their historical abundance. More than for any other indicator, this goal is a judgment call. Full restoration is impossible in a region of 16 million humans, and scientific knowledge is lacking about what wildlife population levels are adequate to maintain vibrant natural communities, particularly as climate disruption continues. But, as this year's results make clear, even the Scorecard's modest target of returning wildlife populations to a portion of historical abundance is still a distant goal.

Figure 15. Despite recent gains by wolves and chinook salmon, key wildlife populations are well below their historical abundance.

SALMON

High in the Rocky Mountains of Idaho, the largest Pacific salmon, the chinook—also called the king salmon—returns to spawn in its native streams after traveling a thousand river-miles upstream past dams,

Culturally, salmon are at the heart of the Northwest; they inhabit the region more thoroughly than any other animal other than humans

deserts, cities, and farms. If these fish are successful in traversing the Northwest's biggest hydrological artery to the place of their birth, then they have a chance at producing a new generation of kings. The Cascadia Scorecard gauges the health of the chinook salmon by monitoring their numbers as they return to the Bonneville Dam, the lowest on the Columbia River, 146 miles upstream from the river's mouth on the Pacific Ocean.

In 2006, chinook salmon numbers during the spring and summer migration seasons were stronger than they were in 2005. More than 200,000 fish passed the dam. But while the 2006 run represents roughly a 30 percent increase over the previous year, little can be discerned from annual variations in salmon numbers. Natural population dynamics mean that counts vary, on average, by about 40 percent a year. Only long-term monitoring can reveal meaningful trends in the population. And 200,000 returning fish, while good by the standards of the past 25 years, is still a very poor showing in historical terms, representing only about 7 percent of historical abundance. In fact, the true story is even bleaker: *wild* salmon probably return at less than 3 percent of their former numbers. The rest of the returning salmon are hatchery-raised fish, whose numbers are far less meaningful as signals of the region's health.

Culturally, salmon are at the heart of the Northwest; physically, they inhabit the region more thoroughly, perhaps, than any animal other than humans. They sustain dozens of Cascadia's species of birds and marine mammals, not to mention people. Once returning in astonishing numbers to nearly every stream in the region, salmon have dwindled with the decline of their habitat, which has been harmed by the damming of rivers, pollution, conversion of land to agriculture and cities, and clearcut logging.

To better protect salmon, northwesterners can begin restoring critical spawning areas and removing dams that block migratory passages but provide little economic benefit to the region, especially the four on the lower Snake River. It is also crucial to carefully monitor and study the fish. Unfortunately, one of the region's best sources for information on the Columbia salmon, the Fish Passage Center based in Portland, fell victim to political wrangling when Idaho senator Larry Craig eliminated funding for the agency, marking a significant step backward both for protecting the salmon and for accurately measuring the state of Cascadia's health.

ORCAS

Relying on chinook salmon as a principal source of food, the distinctive black-and-white killer whales known as orcas are beloved by north-westerners. Part of their popularity can be attributed to the fact that some of them, the so-called "southern residents," live much of their lives near the cities that line the inland marine waters of Puget Sound and the Georgia Strait.

The orcas have not always been cherished by northwesterners. Though they were considered totemic by native peoples, the orcas were trapped for aquariums and shot by fishermen for many years before they began to gain legal protections in the 1970s. By then the southern resident population was dramatically depressed: roughly 70 orcas remained from a population that once numbered two or three hundred. Spared from direct human attacks, the southern resident population has rebounded, though unevenly, during the following decades. Today, northwesterners no longer shoot or trap orcas, but our lifestyles have created impacts that may be just as deadly.

In the last few years, the number of southern resident orcas had been increasing, after a worrisome decline during the first years of the twenty-first century. But in 2006, the whales suffered another setback. Even as new orca calves were welcomed into the pods, the mortality rates increased and four whales apparently died in 2006. By the end of the year, only 86 orcas remained in the southern resident population, roughly one-third of their historical abundance.

Protecting the orcas and restoring their numbers will take concerted efforts on the part of northwesterners who live nearby. Removing toxic sediments from marine waters—and preventing any infusion of new toxics—will benefit both whales and people. But perhaps most critical to the health of the Northwest's inland marine waters is repairing and installing new infrastructure to manage stormwater runoff. The pollution that sluices off roofs and streets, and that emerges from overloaded sewer lines during rainy periods, is severely threatening the ecological balance of Puget Sound. Washington governor Christine Gregoire is pledging a renewed commitment to restoration, but truly addressing the problems will require a financial commitment measured in the billions of dollars.

Wolves have come to symbolize both the fear and the freedom of the wilderness

WOLVES

Perhaps no creature occupies a more conflicted place in the minds of northwesterners than wolves, which have come to symbolize both the fear and the freedom of the wilderness. Once ranging across nearly every landscape in North America, wolves were systemically eradicated from the western continental United States beginning in the nineteenth century—a process that was completed midway through the twentieth. Their absence set in motion a chain reaction in their former landscapes, ultimately altering the populations of elk, songbirds, riverside trees, and even trout.

In the mid-1990s, federal officials reintroduced a few dozen gray wolves to the wilderness of central Idaho and to Yellowstone National Park. In the decade since, the wolves have flourished, expanding their range and number faster than even the most optimistic projections. By 2006, biologists estimated that there were more than 1,250 wolves in the US Rockies. (Idaho and Montana, whose wolf numbers are counted by the Scorecard, boasted 950 wolves.) These populations may be near their peak, as wolves have likely recolonized most of the good habitat available to them.

As wolves inhabit the wilderness once again, they have begun to spill out into agricultural areas, where conflicts with livestock are becoming increasingly common. In 2006, a record 152 wolves were "controlled"—that is, killed—by wildlife officials after they had attacked domestic livestock. Pioneer wolves are now striking out to find new territories in Oregon, Utah, and Washington. Their prospects in those places will depend on laws that provide wolves with enough shelter to gain a foothold. The best policy for wolves may actually be doing very little: giving them room to roam in the backcountry, while monitoring their numbers and activities. And just as wolves have acted as agents of ecological restoration in Yellowstone, so we can welcome them back to the rest of the Northwest as a means of improving the condition of our wild places. One helpful step would be to reintroduce wolves into Washington's Olympic National Park, which can support an ample population of wolves but is too fragmented from other wildlands for wolves to reach on their own.

CARIBOU

While wolves in the Rockies are ever more successful, mountain caribou continue to struggle. The most endangered large mammal in North America, mountain caribou retain only the barest foothold south of the Canadian border. In the remote Selkirk Mountains of northeast Washington, northern Idaho, and southern British Columbia, one herd of caribou persists, and its precarious numbers are included in the Scorecard as a proxy for the populations of mountain caribou across the northern regions.

In 2006, the Selkirk caribou numbered 37, an increase of 2 over the previous year, but still only about 12 percent of their historical abundance. The caribou are threatened on several sides. Clearcut logging has reduced the number of old-growth trees, which support a species of lichen that the caribou depend on for food. People, especially those on snowmobiles, startle the animals in winter and cause them to expend scarce calories on fleeing through deep snow. And predators such as cougars traverse the hardened snowmobile tracks into the herd's winter range—travel they could not otherwise manage.

Stewardship of the southern herd of caribou will require restoration of their forest home. In the short term it will also require expanding the area designated as protected for the caribou. One valuable step would be to expand Washington's Salmo-Priest Wilderness, at the heart of the caribou's ranges, to include an adjacent 17,585-acre roadless area of national forest in Idaho. Officials can also restrict snowmobile access to the caribou's winter range, a step taken by a federal court in the winter of 2006–7.

SAGE-GROUSE

The greater sage-grouse, a desert-dwelling bird known for its astonishing breeding displays, is one of the best indicators of the health of the Northwest's interior sage deserts. As its name implies, the bird depends on relatively intact sagebrush landscapes, a type of ecosystem heavily degraded by ranching, fencing, invasive species, mining, and off-road vehicles.

When Lewis and Clark traveled through the Columbia Basin, they observed sage-grouse in great numbers

When Lewis and Clark traveled through the Columbia Basin, they observed sage-grouse in great numbers. Today, only two small remnant populations survive in eastern Washington. But in Oregon, where sage habitat is remoter and more intact, sage-grouse numbers are relatively stable. Roughly 47,000 of the birds remain in Oregon, perhaps one-quarter of the species' historical abundance in that state.

Several promising efforts to restore sage-grouse numbers are under way, including restoration (and the banning of cattle) at Hart Mountain National Antelope Refuge in eastern Oregon; a wilderness expansion in the Owyhee region of southwestern Idaho; and the conversion of much of the Washington's Hanford Nuclear Reservation to protected conservation areas.

The five wildlife species tracked by the Scorecard average only 18 percent of their historical abundance, and there are manifold reasons to be concerned about their future. All five species face a range of threats, some specific to their habitats but others more general, including climate change and other rising human impacts on natural systems.

Even the most promising trend in the wildlife indicator, the rapid increase in Rocky Mountain wolves, deserves an asterisk. Wolf numbers are still at only a tiny fraction (probably less than 10 percent) of their population prior to European contact, and a wolf-unfriendly policy environment will likely bring a reduction in their numbers in coming years. Meanwhile, the indicator's most precarious species, the Selkirk caribou, the last caribou to visit the continental United States, are in real danger of extirpation.

Preserving native wildlife and restoring them to abundance will require policy choices that provide the animals with the conditions they need to flourish. In some cases this simply means habitat conservation, such as setting aside relatively undisturbed land for sage-grouse or caribou. But in cases like salmon and orcas, where their marine ecosystems are intimately intertwined with human activity, the fixes will be broader and costlier. The good news is that restoring the region's waters would bring a host of benefits to Cascadia's people as well as to its wildlife.

7. POLLUTION

The Score: Unknown. The only Scorecard indicator with no trendline.

The Story: Evidence from multiple sources—including Sightline's 2004 analysis of Cascadians' breastmilk—makes it clear that we carry dangerous, persistent toxics in our bodies. Levels of at least two of these may be rising over time. To reduce contamination, Cascadians can work to clean up polluted sites and to prevent the widespread use of untested chemicals.

The Cascadia Scorecard's pollution indicator measures the concentration of two long-lived toxic chemicals—PCBs and PBDEs—in human bodies, as manifested in mother's milk. Although a complete new set of data are not yet available to update this indicator, a mosaic of related evidence about these compounds and another salient hazard, methyl mercury, suggests no dramatic change in contamination levels in the last several years; levels of PBDEs and mercury may be rising, however.

It's the most intimate kind of pollution: an assortment of dozens, perhaps hundreds, of industrial chemicals that permeate the body of every Cascadian. Most of these substances, which are present only in tiny amounts, didn't even exist a hundred years ago, and their effects on human health are typically unknown. Many may be harmless. But some are not.

Of those proven hazardous, some of the most disturbing are called *persistent bioaccumulative toxics:* that is, they are toxic, they are very slow to break down, and they build up in living tissue over time.

The best-known chemical in this class is probably the pesticide DDT, which was banned in the 1970s. DDT levels in the food chain—and in Cascadians' bodies—have been slowly declining.

But two other persistent bioaccumulative toxics are at potentially dangerous levels: PCBs (polychlorinated biphenyls) and PBDEs (polybrominated diphenyl ethers). In 2004, Sightline investigated the levels of these two compounds in Cascadians' bodies by testing breastmilk samples from 40 first-time mothers with young infants. The findings were alarming: every sample was contaminated with both compounds, at a median of 134 parts per billion of PCBs and 50 parts per billion of PBDEs. The latter was especially striking—the PBDE levels are some 40 times higher than are typically found in northern Europe or Japan. (Breastmilk was tested because it is high in the fats to which PCBs and PBDEs adhere; it can be collected noninvasively; and results can serve as a proxy for the toxic levels, or "body burdens," of similarly aged men and nonbreastfeeding women. Note that these findings do not alter the fact that breastmilk is overwhelmingly considered the healthiest food for infants.)

PCBs are still ubiquitous in soils, sediments, and living things

PCBs, once prized for their stability and resistance to degradation, are now known to impair mammals' nervous and immune systems, and possibly to stunt children's growth. The longevity that made these chemicals so useful to industry also makes them a menace when released into the environment. Though banned in the 1970s, PCBs are still ubiquitous in soils, sediments, and living things. Because the compounds are attracted to fats, they concentrate at each successive link in the food chain, reaching high levels in top predators such as orcas and humans. Puget Sound, with its history of industry and manufacturing, is today a hot spot for PCB contamination. In March 2006, the Washington Department of Health took the unusual step of warning consumers to limit consumption of chinook salmon from Puget Sound to one meal per week, in part because of the high levels of PCBs. (The fish also contain high levels of mercury.) Chinook salmon tested from Puget Sound had up to six times more PCBs than chinook caught elsewhere on the West

Coast. Levels of PCBs in the environment have declined somewhat since their manufacture was banned, but the compounds have left an abiding legacy of contamination that still haunts Cascadia.

PBDEs are flame retardants that until recently were commonly used in furniture foams, and are still present in some new home electronics. These compounds are close chemical cousins to PCBs, and share many of the same properties: they are slow to break down once released into the environment, and can impair neurological development and immune-system functioning in laboratory animals. High levels of PBDEs and PCBs have even been correlated with reduced genital size in polar bears. PBDE concentrations have been on the rise throughout most of the industrial world for decades, with the highest concentrations found in North America. In the human inhabitants of Cascadia, PBDE contamination is now universal. Roughly one-third of the breastmilk samples showed higher levels of PBDEs than PCBs, suggesting that the health threats from PBDEs may gradually overtake those from PCBs.

By every indication, the rapid rise in PBDE concentration over the past several decades has not yet reversed. A 2006 analysis of chemical contamination in the blood of ten Washington residents found PBDEs in every sample, at concentrations comparable to those in the 2004 breastmilk samples. PBDE levels in people's bodies have been linked both to diet (animal products) and to household exposure (house dust). Based on limited tests in California and Canada, concentrations appear to be higher in children than in adults.

Despite this gloomy news, the story of PBDEs is in part hopeful: jurisdictions throughout North America have begun to take a more precautionary approach toward the compounds. The production of the most troubling forms of PBDEs has now ceased in North America, due to an agreement between the US Environmental Protection Agency and the chemicals' manufacturer. A bill passed in Oregon in 2005 banned the use of the most toxic forms of PBDEs in the state; the ban took effect last year. Likewise, Canada announced in 2006 that it would add all forms of PBDEs to its national list of toxic substances, which may make them subject to additional regulations. In Washington, the state health and ecology agencies recommended a total ban of the compounds, and in early 2007 the Washington legislature voted overwhelmingly to follow the departments' recommendations.

If bans of PBDEs prove effective, Cascadians can have hope that PBDE concentrations in the region's environment will gradually wane. But more importantly, we may learn to take more initiative in combating toxics, by requiring that potentially hazardous compounds be tested for safety before they are used widely—and before they enter our bodies.

Although the Cascadia Scorecard tracks only PCBs and PBDEs, other pollutants warrant attention. For example, methyl mercury—the most hazardous form of mercury—can harm the nervous system and is especially dangerous to young children and developing fetuses. Frighteningly, some researchers estimate that as many as 1 in 7 children born in the United States have enough mercury in their blood to reduce their IQ. Much of the mercury that contaminates northwesterners' bodies comes from our diets, particularly seafood, in which mercury contamination is widespread. A recent study by scientists from Oregon State University, for example, found methyl mercury contamination in freshwater fish throughout the American West, with the highest concentrations found among species at the top of the aquatic food chain. The researchers urged pregnant women and children to follow federal health guidelines when making decisions about fish consumption.

But calls for consumer restraint, while important, place the burden of precaution on the victims of contamination rather than on the polluters. Some 70 percent of the methyl mercury in seafood is released by human activities, with the chief North American culprit being coal-fired power plants (such as the Centralia plant in Washington and the Boardman plant in Oregon). Stopping such pollution at the source is the best—and perhaps only—long-term solution to mercury contamination in the food chain.

CONCLUSION:
MIXED SIGNALS

Four important lessons emerge from the 2007 edition of the Cascadia Scorecard.

First, *Cascadians' energy consumption is stuck in high gear.* This is the Scorecard trend most in need of redirection. The long-term threat posed by northwesterners' energy consumption, and by associated climate-changing emissions, is among the most daunting challenges the region faces. Our overdependence on fossil fuels and electricity poses a severe and broad-ranging danger to the natural inheritance that should be our children's birthright.

Making meaningful reductions in energy consumption is a challenge, but a surmountable one. Fortunately, making progress in energy efficiency will have compounding benefits for both humans and nature. Greater efficiency would improve financial security by reducing spending on costly energy imports—money that otherwise could boost the region's job market. Likewise, reducing energy use would reduce toxic emissions from vehicles and power plants, improving health in the process. Exchanging trips in a car for trips on foot, bicycles, or transit would help keep us active and fit, further improving health. So the most important step we can take to reduce Cascadians' impacts on nature will—almost inadvertently—yield compounding benefits for humans as well.

Second, *British Columbia's performance on the Scorecard is substantially better than that of the Northwest states.* Excluding wildlife trends, which are difficult to apportion among the different parts of Cascadia, BC is far closer to "model" performance, and is advancing more quickly, than the US portion of the region (see Figure 16). The province experienced particularly rapid gains during the latter half of the 1990s, when each of the province's trends was improving.

British Columbia's relative success stems, in large part, from factors that have a domino effect, tipping the scales toward progress in several areas at once. For example, BC's comprehensive system of health insurance boosts life expectancy, particularly by offering preventive medical treatments that can forestall the onset of serious illness. At the same time, comprehensive health care helps prevent births from accidental and unwanted pregnancies, by providing a full range of affordable fertility and contraceptive services. And universal health insurance even boosts economic security, by reducing the chance that unforeseen medical expenses will force families into poverty. As a result, the province's health care system has concurrent benefits for

Figure 16.
British Columbia leads
the way in performance
on Scorecard trends.

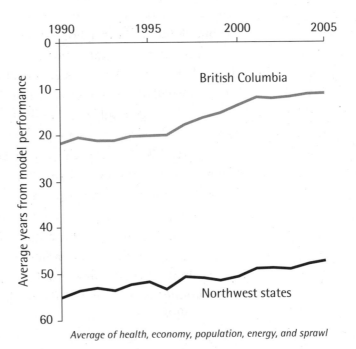

Average of health, economy, population, energy, and sprawl

its residents' health, population levels, and economic security—and it provides them at a lower total cost than does the spottier health care system in the Northwest states.

British Columbia's transportation system may give the province a similar edge over its neighbors to the south. Measured per capita, the province has far fewer miles of roads, streets, and highways than do the Northwest states. Roads—particularly highways leading from central cities to the outskirts of town—facilitate dispersed, sprawling development, which in turn increases fuel use, amplifies the rates of injuries and deaths from car crashes, and sacrifices farmland and forests on the urban fringe. So even though residents of British Columbia make most trips by car, just like their counterparts in the Northwest states, the province's smaller road budget has improved its score in sprawl, energy, and health—all while saving billions of dollars in transportation costs.

Some caution about British Columbia's Scorecard performance is warranted. For example, birthrates in the province are well below the Scorecard model; on average, women in British Columbia have fewer children than those in northern Europe. This may signal a conscious choice by the province's women to have fewer children, but it may also indicate that families are planning fewer births than they might prefer. Some evidence suggests that economic strains, such as housing costs that are rising far faster than incomes, may have made child rearing too much of a financial stretch for some of British Columbia's young families. If so, the province's trend toward smaller families may cast its Scorecard progress in a somewhat different light, narrowing the province's apparent advantage over the Northwest states.

A third lesson taught by the Scorecard is that *most human inhabitants of the region are doing fairly well, but many natural systems are not.* Life expectancy in Cascadia is rising, and is on a par with that of the top tier of industrialized nations. Economic security and fertility patterns have made few advances in recent decades, but are still reasonably close to achieving "model" performance.

The gradual creation of healthy, lasting prosperity is not merely possible, it is already under way

The status of the region's poor, however, is a sad exception to this rule. Poverty in the region has proven to be persistent, even in places where public support for impoverished families is most generous. Today, at least 1 child in 6 lives in poverty in Cascadia. To make genuine headway on this issue, the region must focus its attention on alleviating the conditions that entrap people in poverty. Washington's recent extension of health care coverage to more than half of its children who currently lack health insurance is a step in the right direction, as it provides a safety net for families facing unexpected (and unaffordable) medical expenses.

But in contrast to the relatively high level of well-being experienced by most Cascadians, the Scorecard reveals that the region's natural heritage is in a more precarious position. The three indicators that most directly measure impacts on nature (sprawl, energy, and wildlife) are all further from their targets than the indicators that measure human wellbeing. Per-person energy consumption remains stuck at a high plateau. Sprawl remains the norm in Cascadia's cities, and continues to take its toll on the farms and open spaces at the urban fringe. And each of the wildlife species tracked by the Scorecard—including those that are rebounding thanks to northwesterners' improving stewardship—is severely depressed from its historical abundance. Fortunately, despite the many threats the region's natural systems face, opportunities for restoration abound.

The fourth and final lesson we can glean from this year's Scorecard is that **there is reason for optimism.** The gradual creation of healthy, lasting prosperity is not merely possible, it is already under way. Progress is slower than we might hope, and it is not evident in every trend. Yet taken together, the gradual, decades-long rise in our average Scorecard performance shows that we Cascadians can prosper, and our well-being can improve, even as our place regains more of its lost natural riches.

The Scorecard's real-world models show that further gains are possible. As a result, the Scorecard offers a practical vision for a more prosperous place, where prosperity is defined not merely by our finances, but by our shared values: healthy people living in strong communities, governed by a vigorous democracy, and exercising responsible stewardship for our shared natural bounty. If Cascadia can approach model performance on each of its Scorecard indicators, it can position itself as a model for the world—not only as a place that can shine in one narrow realm, but as a place where both people and nature are thriving, regenerating, and renewing themselves.

ACKNOWLEDGMENTS

Cascadia Scorecard 2007: Seven Key Trends Shaping the Future of the Northwest was written by Clark Williams-Derry, Eric de Place, and Alan Thein Durning, with assistance from research consultants John Abbotts and Jessica Branom-Zwick and research intern Deric Gruen. Staff members Elisa Murray, Leigh Sims, and Anna Fahey provided invaluable insights and assistance with editing and production. We thank those who assisted with the creation of the maps in this volume, including CommEn Space staff Chris Davis and Erica Simek, who designed the maps of life expectancy and fertility; Matt Stevenson of CORE GIS, who designed the maps of climate change and sprawl; Sheila Martin and Erik Rundell from Portland State University, who provided data from which the Measure 37 claims map was derived; and Josiah Mault and Philip Mote from the Office of the Washington State Climatologist, who provided the data for the climate change map, and technical advice on its interpretation. We thank editor Nick Allison for his thorough and much-needed revisions to the text; book designer Jennifer Shontz for her insight and skill; and proofeader Sherri Schultz for her attention to detail.

We are grateful to our many volunteers for their valuable contributions in 2006 and early 2007, including communications interns Mackenzie Berg, Danielle Burhop, and Nick Neely; development interns Faye Conte, Erin Frost, Caitlin McKee, Felicia Merritt, and Erica Peters; grants intern Amanda Gibson; leadership intern Amy Chan; and many other volunteers who donated time and skills, including Marcia Baker, Yoram Bauman, Laura Bentley, Eric Berman, Erik Bluemel, David Boctor, Curtis Carpenter, Jennifer Covert, Isobel Davis, Keri Detore, Megan Griffiths, Deb Guenther,

Jack Guenther, Kate Guenther, Kelly Guenther, Natalie Gulsrud, Sebastian Helm, Rosemarie Ives, Lynn Jordan, Nathan Karres, David Kershner, Katherine Killebrew, Mark Kotzer, Adam Kramer, Matt Leber, David Manelski, Andrew Martin, Rick Martinez, Laurel Minter, Aileen Murphy, Greg Nickels, Shannon Perry, Sean Porter, Laura Puckett and Bill Bromberg at DLA Piper, Andrea Riseden-Perry, John Roberts, Sarah Salkin, Glenn Thomas, Mark Trahant, TJ Williams, Jr., and Seth Zuckerman. We are also grateful to the experts who helped with the development of Tidepool, including David Beers, Lark Corbeil, Chip Giller, Scott Miller, Eileen Quigley, and Sam Tucker.

We thank the partners and experts who peer-reviewed Sightline's work or assisted with outreach in 2006, including Amy Baernstein, Jon Barrett, Tim Buckley, Elaine Clegg, Minot Cleveland, Noelle Dobson, Lawrence Frank, Governor Chris Gregoire, Trevor Hancock, Cheeying Ho, Kristin Jacobsen, Hilary Karasz, Michael McGinn, David Levinger, Todd Litman, Evan Manvel, Mary Kyle McCurdy, Michael Mortensen, Gordon Price, Jessyn Schor, and Rob Zako. We also thank volunteer blog contributors John Abbotts, Kathryn Maly, Dan Staley, and Arie van der Hoeven; and those in Oregon who contributed their time and stories to our research on Measure 37, including Don and Deanna Dean, Laurel and Brian Hines, David and Kathy Jones, Suzie Kunzman, Scott Lay, Jim and Sandy LeTourneux, and Crystal and Bob Vanderzanden; and also Eric Stachon. And we extend a special thank-you to Colleen Kaleda and Dana Brown.

Sightline thanks its board of directors for their donation of much time and support: board chair John Atcheson, and board members Alan Thein Durning, Jeff Hallberg, Bill Kramer, Ethan Meginnes, Gordon Price, Allen Puckett, Laura Retzler, Valerie Tarico, and David Yaden. We also thank our trustees, Jeanette Henderson, Erik Jansen, Ann Martin, John Savage, and Chris Troth, as well as former board member Gail

Achterman, who completed her service in 2006 and now serves the organization as an advisor.

Finally, Sightline is grateful to its hardworking staff: senior researcher Eric de Place, development director Peter Drury, executive director Alan Thein Durning, communications strategist Anna Fahey, director of strategic initiatives Christine Hanna, Tidepool editor Kristin Kolb, communications director Elisa Murray, grants associate Madeline Ostrander, senior development associate Stacey Panek, executive assistant and office administrator Meighan Pritchard, senior communications associate Leigh Sims, and research director Clark Williams-Derry. We also thank former finance and operations manager Amy Zimerman for her service to the organization.

OUR SUPPORTERS

CASCADIA STEWARDS COUNCIL

We wish to express particular appreciation for members of the Cascadia Stewards Council, comprising those who have made multiyear financial commitments at a level of $1,000 annually, or greater. The complete membership is listed, here, in descending order of total 2006 giving, with Founding Members of the Council featured with an asterisk (*). By making multiyear major gift commitments, these donors enable Sightline to plan strategically and work responsibly.

Tom & Sonya Campion*
Contorer Foundation*
Christopher & Mary Troth*
Judy Pigott*
Valerie Tarico & Brian Arbogast
Jabe Blumenthal & Julie Edsforth*
Loeb/Meginnes Foundation*
Linda S. Park & Denis G. Janky*
Magali & Jeffrey Belt*
Janet Vogelzang & Mark Cliggett*
Jeff & Nicole Hallberg*
Harvey Jones & Nancy Iannucci
Laura Retzler & Henry Wigglesworth*
Maggie Hooks & Justin Ferrari*
Amy & Alan Thein Durning*
David Callahan*
Gun & Tom Denhart*
Mary A. Crocker Trust (for Elizabeth Atcheson)*
Mary Fellows & John Russell*
John Atcheson*
Jeremy & Karen Mazner*
Jonathan Durning & Melanie Ronai*
Allen & Laura Puckett
Gail L. Achterman*
Gretchen & Erik Jansen*
Kristayani & Jerry Jones*
Mark Groudine & Cynthia Putnam*
Janice & David Yaden*

Jeanette Henderson & Andrew Behm*
Tom & Jennifer Luce*
Doane Rising
Edward Mills & Irene Pasternack*
Glenn S. Rodriguez & Molly E. R. Keating*
Maria & Peter Drury
Pete & Joeve Wilkinson
Anirudh Sahni*
Jeff Youngstrom & Becky Brooks*
JF & Leslie Baken*
Paul & Donna Balle*
Connie Battaile*
Tony & Sue Beeman*
Anonymous*
Anonymous
Thomas Buxton & Terri Anderson*
Jon Carder & Monique Baillargeon*
Vincent Celie & Aileen Murphy
Ann & Doug Christensen*
Grace K. Dinsdale
Peter Donaldson & Cynthia Yost*
John & Jane Emrick*
Maradel Krummel Gale*
Christine Hanna & Eugene Pitcher*
Anonymous
Mark Kotzer & Lauren Adler*
Bill Kramer & Melissa Cadwallader*
David Lahaie & Petra Franklin Lahaie

Langdon Marsh & Ellie Putnam*
Sara Moorehead & Jeff Ratté*
Linda Moulder & Jerry White
Tanya & Patrick Niemeyer
Jean Marie Piserchia & Robert C. Ball*
James & Rebecca Potter*
Gordon Price & Len Sobo*

Ingrid Rasch*
Mike & Faye Richardson
Abbe Sue Rubin
Dan Sewell & Susie Callahan
Manya & Howard Shapiro*
Sonya M. Stoklosa
Birgitte B. Williams*

2006 DONORS

Gifts were received from January 1 through December 31, 2006, and donors are listed in descending order of gift amount.

We wish to pay special tribute to two faithful donors who died in 2006, Dr. George Saslow and one who wished to remain anonymous (and was, in fact, our very first major donor). They each had tremendous confidence and hope in the future of Cascadia, and lived inspirational lives of dedication to the principles of sustainability. Their legacy is woven into Sightline's future.

$200,000 and above
Washington Progress Alliance

$100,000 to $199,999
The Russell Family Foundation

$50,000 to $99,999
The Bullitt Foundation
Glaser Progress Foundation
Wallace Global Fund

$25,000 to $49,999
Social Venture Partners
Voter Action Fund of Tides Foundation
Tom & Sonya Campion (Campion Foundation)
Quixote Foundation
Contorer Foundation
Carolyn Foundation

$10,000 to $24,999
Maryanne & David Tagney Jones
Creative Strategies (Kurt Guenther)
Aveda

Judy Pigott
Valerie Tarico & Brian Arbogast
Jabe Blumenthal & Julie Edsforth
Howard & Troth Family Fund
Loeb/Meginnes Foundation
Northwest Area Foundation
Linda S. Park & Denis G. Janky
Mark & Susan Torrance
Microsoft (Matching Gift Program)

$5,000 to $9,999
Harvey Jones & Nancy Iannucci
The Kongsgaard-Goldman Foundation
Maggie & Doug Walker
Laura Retzler & Henry Wigglesworth
Christopher & Mary Troth

$2,500 to $4,999
Anonymous
Magali & Jeffrey Belt
Janet Vogelzang & Mark Cliggett
Maggie Hooks & Justin Ferrari
Amy & Alan Thein Durning

David Callahan
Robert & Judy Fisher
Gun & Tom Denhart
Jubitz Family Foundation
Mary A. Crocker Trust (for Elizabeth Atcheson)
Mary Fellows & John Russell

$1,001 to $2,499

Jeff & Nicole Hallberg
John Atcheson
Anonymous
Jeremy & Karen Mazner
Jonathan Durning & Melanie Ronai
Allen & Laura Puckett
Carrie & Barry Saxifrage
Gail L. Achterman
Amgen Foundation (Matching Gift Program)
Erin & Jonathan Becker
Lowell & Nancy Ericsson
Gretchen & Erik Jansen
Kristayani & Jerry Jones
Mark Groudine & Cynthia Putnam
Smiling Dog Foundation
Janice & David Yaden
Jeanette Henderson & Andrew Behm
Tom & Jennifer Luce
Doane Rising
Marvin & Jean Durning
Edward Mills & Irene Pasternack
Glenn S. Rodriguez & Molly E. R. Keating
Maria & Peter Drury
Pete & Joeve Wilkinson
Anirudh Sahni
Eco Encore
Jeff Youngstrom & Becky Brooks

$1,000

JF & Leslie Baken
Paul & Donna Balle
Connie Battaile

Tony & Sue Beeman
Anonymous (2)
Thomas Buxton & Terri Anderson
Jon Carder & Monique Baillargeon
Vincent Celie & Aileen Murphy
Ann & Doug Christensen
Grace K. Dinsdale
Peter Donaldson & Cynthia Yost
John & Jane Emrick
Maradel Krummel Gale
Christine Hanna & Eugene Pitcher
Bob & Betty Hawkins
Robert & Phyllis Henigson
Anonymous
David Kaplan
Jean Walden Kershner
Mark Kotzer & Lauren Adler
Bill Kramer & Melissa Cadwallader
David Lahaie & Petra Franklin Lahaie
Clemens & Marilyn Laufenberg
William & Emmy Lawrence
Matt & Leslie Leber
Ruth & Terry Lipscomb
Timothy Londergan
Anonymous
Langdon Marsh & Ellie Putnam
Sara Moorehead & Jeff Ratté
Linda Moulder & Jerry White
Tanya & Patrick Niemeyer
Jean Marie Piserchia & Robert C. Ball
James & Rebecca Potter
Gordon Price & Len Sobo
Ingrid Rasch
Reeve Family Foundation
Mike & Faye Richardson
Abbe Sue Rubin
John & Lorrie Schleg
Dan Sewell & Susie Callahan
Manya & Howard Shapiro
Sonya M. Stoklosa

Steve & Liann Sundquist
Washington Health Foundation
Washington Mutual (Matching Gift Program)
Birgitte B. Williams
Winky Foundation

$500 to $999

DeeAnn Dougherty & Paul Raether
Yoram K. Bauman
Wilburforce Foundation
Carol D. Roberts
Anonymous
Matt Griffin
David Huffaker & Barbara Staley
Neil Kelly, Inc.
Kristin K. Martinez
Donald & Pamela Mitchell
Ann Parker-Way & Paul Way
John Wedgwood & Kathleen Turner
Kathryn E. Wilbur

$250 to $499

Richard Meyer & Aleta Howard
Curtis DeGasperi & Sara Waterman
Kenneth G. Zick & Yvonne M. Zick

Peter & Rita Thein
T. William & Beatrice Booth
Fred Miller & Karla Wenzel
ShoreBank Enterprise Pacific
Ralph U. Klose
Vincent Houmes
John & Hanna Liv Mahlum Trust
Leonard E. Pavelka
Scott & C. Joan Sandberg
George Thornton & Lee Miller
Wendy Green
Ann De Lancey & Nelson Fausto
Matthew Fingerhut & Susie Frazier
Albert E. Foster
Heather & Bruce Johnson
Frances & David Korten
Bronwyn & Brian Scott
Kristopher & Jo Ann Townsend
Willie Weir & Kat Marriner
Thor Hinckley & Alison Wiley

Sightline is grateful to the approximately 400 additional individuals, organizations, and families who also made gifts in 2006.

IN-KIND DONATIONS

We are grateful to the following individuals and organizations who donated valuable services or material gifts to Sightline in 2006.

John Atcheson
Yoram K. Bauman
Bill Blosser
Cameron Catering
Cupcake Royale
Dinette
Peter Donaldson
John Ewald
Lawrence Frank
Maradel Krummel Gale
Gelatiamo
Georgetown Brewing
Michel Girard
Kurt Guenther (Creative Strategies)
IslandWood
David Lahaie & Petra Franklin Lahaie
Ann Martin
Karen & Jeremy Mazner

Bill McKibben
Mithun
Nau
QFC
Laura Retzler & Henry Wigglesworth
Doane Rising
Melanie Ronai & Jonathan Durning
Richard & Jileen Russell
Lura Smith & Bill Shubach
Sam Sullivan
Sierra Brewing
Glenn Thomas
Tides Canada Foundation
Trader Joe's
Karla Wenzel & Fred Miller
Vulcan, Inc.
David & Janice Yaden